KEEPING MINIBEASTS

STICK INSECTS

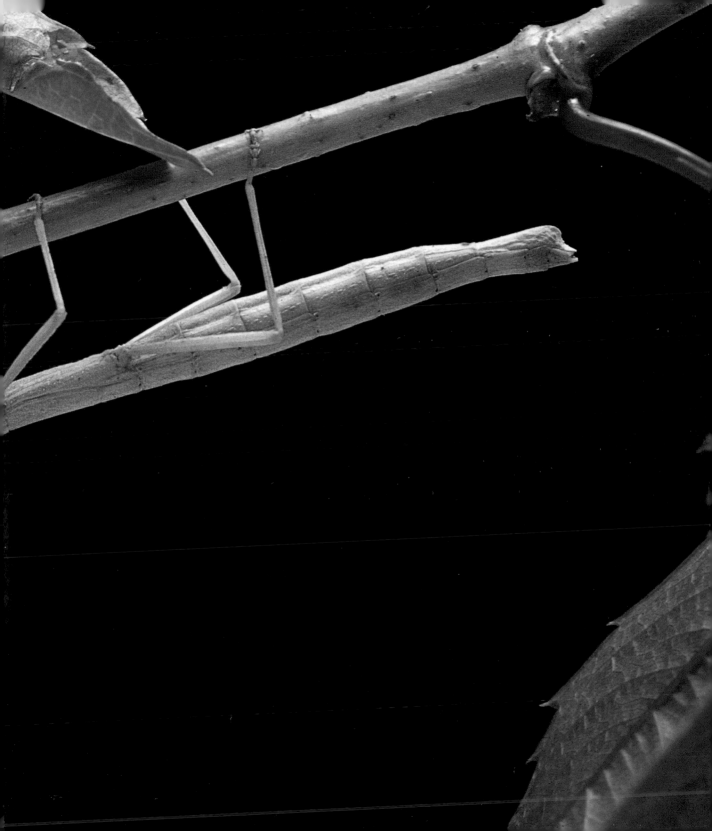

© 1991 Franklin Watts

Franklin Watts, Inc.
387 Park Avenue South
New York, N.Y. 10016

Editor: Hazel Poole
Design: K and Co
Consultant: Michael Chinery

Library of Congress Cataloging-in-Publication Data

Watts, Barrie.
      Stick insects/text and photographs, Barrie Watts.
         p. cm.–(Keeping minibeasts)
      Includes index.
      Summary: Discusses the housing, breeding, feeding and special
needs of stick insects and mantises when kept as pets.
    ISBN 0-531-14220-5
    1. Stick insects as pets – Juvenile literature.   2. Praying
mantises as pets – Juvenile literature.   3. Stick insects – Juvenile
literature.   4. Praying mantis – Juvenile literature.   [1. Stick
insects as pets.   2. Praying mantises as pets.]   I. Title.
II. Series.   91–12283
SF459.S74W38   1992   CIP
638'.5724–dc20   AC

Printed in Italy by G. Canale & C. S.p.A. - Borgaro T.se - Torino

KEEPING MINIBEASTS

STICK INSECTS

Text and Photographs: Barrie Watts

CONTENTS

Franklin Watts

New York • London • Toronto • Sydney

Introduction

Stick insects are large insects that live in trees and bushes. Some are long and thin, while others are fat and spiny. As with all insects, their shape and size is determined by their need to breed and survive in the environment in which they live. They are easy to keep and can be bought from pet shops or through mail order.

Stick insects are masters of camouflage. Some of them resemble dead twigs, while others look like leaves and flowers. This important feature helps them to survive in their habitat. It prevents them from being eaten by predators and also enables them to catch their own prey easily.

They are all normally slow-moving and if disturbed will keep still, making it less likely that they will be spotted by predators.

Mantises

Stick insects, and the closely-related leaf insects, which are very flat and leaflike, are vegetarian and eat the leaves of the plants they live on. Mantises have large eyes and are very efficient at spotting the movement of a possible

meal. They are often quite colorful since many of them look like the flower of the plant they live on. Mantises are fierce predators and the female sometimes eats the male after she has mated with him.

Stick insects live in all the warmer parts of the world, especially in warm, humid jungles. The tropical areas are the best habitats for them and many strange and interesting species can be found. In the United States, stick insects are found mainly in the South.

Housing

The best way to keep stick insects at home is in clear plastic pet cages or fish tanks. If the containers are clear you will be able to see the insects easily without disturbing them. Normally

they are active at night and during the day they are still. They are more likely to breed if they are not disturbed. Line the bottom of the cage with paper towel as this can easily be changed when it gets dirty.

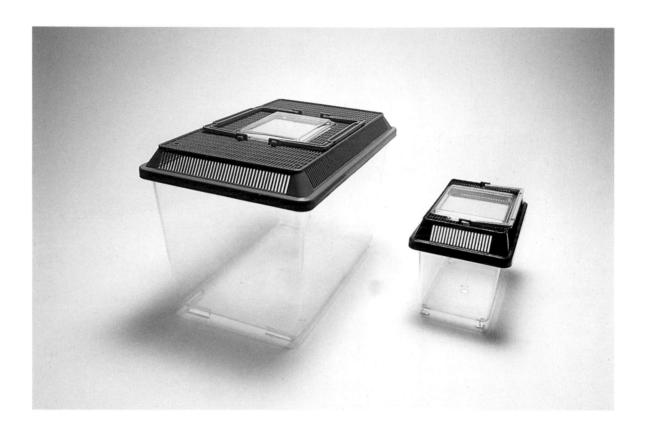

A tall, plastic cage will be big enough to house about four or five stick insects. Many stick insects will live quite happily on a warm sunny windowsill out of direct sunlight. The height of the cage is important as the stick insects need to hang while they are changing their skins.

Those from the tropical parts of the world require warmth and humidity, so they are more difficult to keep at home. Start with the easy ones first and move on to others later.

Indian spiny stick insects are easy to breed at home. You will need at least one female and two or three males to start with.

Keep them at 68°/77°F and give them a fresh
supply of food each day. When the females are
ready to lay their eggs, they will often just drop
them onto the floor of the cage. In order for the
eggs to hatch, gently pick them up and put them
on some sand in a small box. Leave them in the
warm adult cage.

Stick insects feed on many different types of leaves. Oak, hazelnut, grapevine and rhododendron leaves can be used to feed most stick insects. Small twigs with leaves can be cut and put into jars of wet sand to keep them fresh.

When changing the leaves, be careful not to pull the insects off their food because their legs are fragile and are easily damaged.

Praying mantises feed on live insects only and so are more difficult to keep. Crickets and grasshoppers are a good food for the larger mantises and they can often be bought from pet stores. Flies can be hatched from anglers maggots. They can be kept in a tightly sealed container in a refrigerator. When they are cold they cannot fly so will not escape. An adult mantis will eat many flies each day so you will need a good supply of them.

Life cycle

The female stick insect often drops her eggs during the night. She may produce up to nine of these each day and is able to keep this up for several weeks. If she doesn't mate with a male she is still able to lay eggs that will hatch. These eggs will produce female nymphs only. This often happens because males are quite rare.

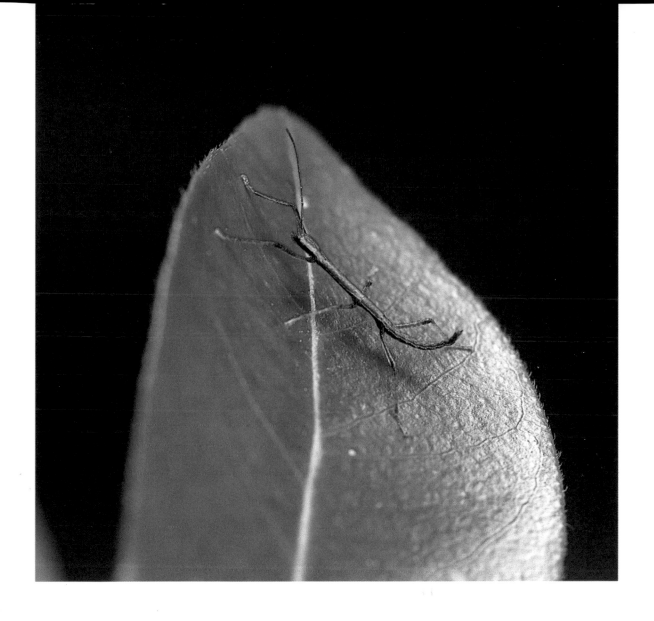

The eggs can take 200 days to hatch and when the baby nymphs emerge they are less than one half inch long.

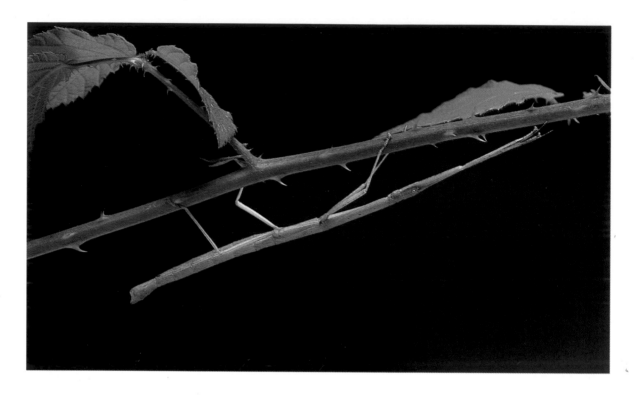

The young nymphs spend about 130 days maturing into adult insects. During this time they change their skin five or six times. It is important not to handle the insects at this time as they are very soft and can be easily damaged. To escape danger, they become motionless or pretend they are dead and drop to the ground.

The giant spiny stick insect's eggs can take up to 20 months to hatch.

Praying mantises lay their eggs in a foam capsule. When they hatch, the tiny nymphs often eat each other.

Some species of stick insect frighten predators by rapidly opening their brightly colored wings.

Mantises catch their prey with a pair of spiny front legs. These legs shoot out rapidly in order to grab their victim. The spines give the mantises a good grip on their prey.

Index